EATING TURTLE

Small Harbor Publishing

Cover art: Liz Williams
Interior design: Brianna Chapman
Editor: Sarah Mengel
Publisher: Allison Blevins
Director: Kristiane Weeks-Rogers

EATING TURTLE
ALEXIS STRATTON
ISBN 978-1-957248-47-9
Harbor Editions,
an imprint of Small Harbor Publishing

EATING TURTLE

Alexis Stratton

Harbor Editions
Small Harbor Publishing

To all those who helped me feel at home when I was far from it,
and to N. and E., who gave me a safe place to land

CONTENTS

EATING TURTLE

IN THE SHADOW OF THE TAJ

Monkeys chasing each other across rooftops.

The smoke from your cigarette.

The curtain of the night falling behind the Taj, its shadowy silhouette.

God is close.

Allah moves across the face of the stone, never seen, but always present.

Prayers called up to the night sky, shouted and sung from speakers like megaphones, echoing across Agra at sunset.

You say you wish they'd be quiet. That prayers are meant to be whispered, shared only between you and God.

A chorus of prayers.

A family of monkeys. A mother sliding down a wall to scoop up her child, who looks too afraid to climb.

In the street, a little girl plays with a yellow balloon, dodging motorbikes and the big, dark puddle in the middle of her street.

You tell me the Taj was more beautiful years ago. That now the pollution gets in the way.

You tell me not all Indian men are like what they say but to be careful in Delhi.

You tell me about a French woman you took to dinner and showed around for three days and how she asked you to come see her in France and how, when her plane finally left, you couldn't believe she was gone.

How you refused your family's proposals for arranged marriages, put it off by getting degree after degree, and finally just said, "No." You were sent out from your family's home. You only talk to your mother now, occasionally. Still, your younger brothers can't get married until you do.

You say we are different. We are both different. That's why you talk to me. That people here all go in one direction, but you go the other.

You believe in God but are not religious. When a bell rings—a Hindu sign for good luck—you don't pray like your friend, but you place your fist to your chest and then to your lips, the same thing my friend did whenever we passed a Hindu temple on the road.

You say we are all connected. That race and religion can't keep us apart. We are different, but we are connected.

*

You ask me when I cut my hair, when I started dressing like a man.

"Did something happen?"

Did something happen?

How could I explain the sense of awakening which allowed me to become who I am? The sensation the first time I wore a bowtie? The feeling of being at home in my own skin?

There aren't words for that kind of letting go. How it felt like holding my younger self and asking forgiveness for all those years I tried to force them to be someone they were not. How it felt like that younger self snuggled into me and finally relaxed for the first time in a lifetime.

Like chords that finally resolved.

"No, nothing happened," I say. "I just gave myself permission to be who I am."

*

Metal detectors. Gender-segregated pat-downs.

"I'm sorry to ask this, but are you a 'madam' or a 'sir'?" All to tell me which gate to go through to store my bags at the Taj Mahal.

Are you a "madam" or a "sir"?

"It's smart you travel like this," you say. "Do you dress like this back in the U.S., too?"

I want to say *I have dressed like this my whole life,* but I haven't.

You ask me to join you for dinner, "a place the French girl said didn't even feel like Agra—there is a garden and sparkling lights—" but I don't want to be your next French girl.

*

You say, the next day, you only asked me because in India, it's strange to be alone.

"We think," you say, "if you are alone, you must be lonely. I wanted to help. There are guests who sometimes stay in their rooms for days. In their countries, maybe they just go by themselves and read a book and that's all they want. Here, we ask them if they're okay." You laugh.

You remind me of a man I met in New York, an actor. We were both in our early twenties, and as a friend of a friend, he wanted to show me everything the city had to offer. He asked me to tell him a story, and I did. A week later, he called my dorm room and just wanted to talk.

But also wanted to see me again. Wanted other things, maybe love, maybe some connection—that was there, but wasn't.

An echo of a connection.

A shadow on a wall.

I hung up the phone and didn't call again.

*

I didn't tell you goodbye. Just goodnight, on the roof, as if I would see you again, as if we would keep talking about these things each day.

You speak of learning to value those brief connections.

I want to say my life has been a series of goodbyes.

"Meeting people part," a Korean colleague of mine once said. "Even husband and wife must part someday."

Thin red lines pulled taut between us. Blood and gods, the touch of things unseen. Light changing on the Taj. Wind in leaves. A breath in that we're slowly learning to let go.

TALKING WITH THE DEAD

The Egyptians talked with the dead. Bodies encased in linen, protected by gilded masks, the dead were sought for protection, advice. I imagine their spirits waiting among the tombs for a letter to slip under the door, hieroglyphs freshly drawn across papyrus.

But I'm wrong—they wrote on bowls. On linen. On stone tablets.

Many thought the dead were to blame for the trials of the living. They would write to the dead for peace or forgiveness. They blamed them for misfortune and tried to improve their mood.

Sometimes the dead even responded, it seems. A son writes to his dead mother that she told him to bring her poultry. The son says that he brought his mother seven quails and that she ate them—and then complains about his suffering, about his mother acting against him. In complete indignation, he asks, "Who will pour water for you?"

My junior year of college, when I was studying abroad in Ireland, my friend Rose and I took a trip to Italy. After we'd spent a day visiting

Florence and before we took the train to Pompeii, we decided to go to mass in downtown Rome. We walked into the cathedral—tall, arched, gilded ceiling work above us, our jackets wet from the rain, my book bag heavy on my back. I set my camera on my lap as we sat down.

The service began in Italian, the words unfamiliar but the motions, the place, reminiscent of churches I'd been in before—the hum of the priest's voice, the rhythms of the liturgy. I bowed my head.

And there it was—that incense.

Had I never smelled incense before Paul's death? Had I even been to a Catholic service before I went to that funeral?

And all I could think of was what my best friend Jenny said after the funeral finished—Paul hated incense. He would've hated the incense.

Plaster casts in Pompeii preserve the positions of bodies that decayed in compacted ash. In the 1860s, archaeologists began to discover pockets of air as they were digging and searching, and they realized they'd uncovered cavities where bodies had been. They filled them with plaster.

Now what's left is this: a man's body, writhing in agony, mouth twisted in a final scream. A dog curled around itself. A man and a woman holding tight to each other, waiting for suffocation, those final, precious, horrible moments.

Last night I saw James Cagney die

as Lon Chaney, he spelled out *I love you*

with his hands. His eyes were wry, narrowed,

as if savoring a cigar and a brandy, he spelled out

Forgive me with that keen savoring look,

then his head fell to the side.

—from "Death," Sharon Olds

After Travis died at age fifteen, his white-haired grandfather's lips trembled on stage as he eulogized in a harmonious baritone. "When a wife loses a husband, she's called a widow. When a child loses a parent, he's called an orphan." In his pause, I heard the sniffles from people around me. "There are no words for when a parent loses a child."

Paul's was the last funeral I'd gone to before Travis's. I was working at the Methodist campus ministry at the University of South Carolina, and Travis was the stepbrother of one of the new freshmen. Travis died within the first few months I was working in the ministry—epileptic fit, choking.

It was a time of loss. Another freshman's best friend died the summer before they started college—running along the side of the road, the girl had collapsed—something to do with her heart. She was dead when they found her, lying in a heap by the passing cars.

I was just a year older than they were when Paul died. He was nineteen—cancer, nodes and nodes and nodes of cancer cells, first the hip, then the lungs, then the treatments that didn't work—for two years —then he's bald, then he's pale.

Then he's dead.

In Gyeongju, South Korea, neat paths weave their way between the ancient burial mounds of kings and queens, the soft, round shapes sticking up from the ground like body parts—noses, breasts, elbows pressing into the sky. Inside them: bones, bowls, bracelets, figurines, crowns, cups.

I want to dig into the hundreds of mounds, to scrape and claw until I feel metal and bone against my skin, until I hold the hidden things in my hands and emerge, face smudged, clothing soiled, fingernails filled with dirt.

But I don't. I take a tour inside one instead, looking at the riches they found there, these old things no one needs anymore.

It was always my intention to come clean. To tell my friends that it was my fault Paul died. But words are powerful, and I lacked the courage.

Even years later, I still want to tell them. But I convince myself it's no longer important. That I was young—and really, it's silly to blame myself.

The Ninth Ward was a ghost town, two years after Hurricane Katrina. Unruly grasses climbed up walls of houses, windows dark and empty. Each house was a headstone—a memorial to a family, to someone who had once been, had once been there. Spray paint marked them with glyphs. Roofs slumped like deformed shoulders, siding lay stripped, baring the inner skin—an accidental glimpse of nudity, bared flesh that makes you turn away, ashamed.

Down the street, the levy peered across the land, the remains of people's lives, the city's still streets.

But if we could talk to the dead, what would we say? Would we tell them that we held onto their things and their memories like a child clutches a blanket?

It would be true at first. But then, well, you know how it happens. Days pass, then weeks. We remember less, we excise the daily pain and exchange it for tomorrows—for chores, for driving to and from work, for new love.

And what if the dead have forgotten us? If we could slip a letter under that heavenly door, who's to say they'd ever receive it? That they'd even know who sent it?

In New Orleans, a funeral is a celebration. A funeral brings music and parades.

It begins slow—with low, somber tones played on brass, clarinet, sax. You take step, step, step toward the graveyard. You move your feet, slow, slow. You sway your umbrella with the music.

And then, when the hearse goes on ahead, or maybe once the sadness of the burial is over and the crowd has turned to go home, there is this sudden up tempo. There is dancing—these sad people dancing!—and it is to say *We celebrate your life* or *We're happy to be alive* or *Thank God it wasn't me.*

———∞———

From a diary entry, 10/18/1998

As for me, Homecoming went really well. Paul picked me up at 8:15PM instead of the planned 8:00PM because I got back late from the band competition. This of course was after he had been worrying for the previous 3 weeks I wouldn't be able to go, but I can get into that later. So anyway he picked me up and gave me a corsage (hey, I know I spelled it wrong), and I gave him a boutaneer (also probably spelled wrong). I gave him a white carnation and he gave me a lavender rose. It was beautiful and smelled wonderful.

Mom and Dad (or shall I say Mom—I wasn't worried about Dad) were pretty nice, not too hard on him, at least. Mom took a couple of pictures and we were off. Jameson (Paul's Senior brother) drove us to the HS… The decorations were great! The theme was Hawaiian Luau and some of the decorations were really cool… So Paul and I and our group of friends danced and talked a lot, while my brother threatened bodily harm to Paul to "keep him in line," and overall it was a lot of fun… For the record, I wore a long black dress with a little over-the-shoulders mini-jacket, and Paul wore khakis and a nice shirt.

Well, I know that I have some stories to tell and I promise I'll tell them, but first I have homework to do. Gotta go—

Love,

A

444

Last summer, I checked to make sure I still had it.

In my parents' attic in North Carolina, I was looking through books, re-packing another time for another city, completing the final leg of my move from New Orleans back to South Carolina. I dug through a knee-high box, sweat rolling down my temple to my chin, T-shirt clinging to my stomach and back.

The old planner was sitting on top of *Wheelock's Latin* (one of the books Paul's aunt had given me a few years before), under a Gaelic phrasebook and the thin guidebook I'd bought while in Rome—a picture of the Colosseum filling the front cover.

I held it in my hands, unfastened the snap. The aluminum can tab was right where I'd put it after I pulled it off that can in tenth grade. It hadn't moved—even after I broke up with him that summer before eleventh grade. For whatever reason, before and after the dances, before and after the breakup, before and after the cancer, before and long after his death, I kept this memento of my first boyfriend there, clipped onto one of the planner's binder rings.

I remember we were all sitting around a lunch table—four giggly teenagers. I don't remember the conversation. I don't remember what I ate. I don't even remember which three friends I was sitting with.

What I do remember is this:

Aluminum can in my hands. Running through the alphabet as I pulled and pushed the can tab up and down, hoping to get a P (for Paul) or M (for Miller)—because, like every teenager in that cafeteria, I knew that it meant we'd get married, that the letter the tab popped off on would give me an initial for my future mate. It would be fated in that moment—the crack in the aluminum fastener, the light tug—and there it was.

P—for Paul.

☐

From a diary entry, 10/13/2005—Biloxi, MS

Salvation Army warehouse. Walked there. The streets were littered. Glass shards everywhere. Flies. Strong stench once in awhile. A toy here. A boat along the side of the road called "Good Times." (Later, someone told me they met the owner. He and his dog were on the boat when the storm hit. Owner went unconscious. Awoke on the side of the road, still in the boat.) A stack of photo albums, frames without pictures. Shredded plastic in trees/bushes, flapping like streamers or ticker tape. Video tape strewn about the road, broken VHS's. Broken trees. A tree on a house. Stepping over branches. Power lines down, snaked in the middle of the street. Houses off foundations, shifted into roads, away from front steps. A roof collapsed with nothing retrievable beneath it…

We hold onto things that could never matter to anyone else, that have no inherent value. Perhaps we hold on because, in some way, it brings us closer to the ones we have lost. Perhaps because if we meet the dead again, we want to be able to tell them how faithfully we mourned. Perhaps because we are afraid to forget—because where do the dead reside in this world, if not in memory?

But we will die as well, and then that watch he gave you for your thirtieth anniversary is just a watch, sold at an estate sale, that someone picks up for a deal. Or that Christmas card your grandma sent you with that hand-stitched snowman on the front is just trash—picked up with the rest of it, piled on the curb after the family cleans out your room, salvaging what they can.

⬯

"We seek the absolute everywhere, and only ever find things."

–Novalis, German writer, 1772-1801

We were standing outside of AP Statistics senior year. I don't know what it was—youth, too many TV sitcoms with quippy comebacks—but the words came before I gave them any weight. It reminded me of that time in third grade when I tore a hole in my leggings at recess and said to my friend, "My mom's gonna kill me"—but really, I knew she wouldn't. Really, I was just saying what I'd heard Stephanie or one of the other characters say on *Full House*.

I don't remember it clearly, but I remember that Paul was being annoying. And for some reason, he was swinging around his Calculus textbook. At some point, he swung, and it just missed me and hit my friend Carrie in the head.

I could've just as easily said, "Go to hell," but I was a Christian, and that was the worst thing I could've said. "You die," I said instead, in sarcastic enough of a tone—like a scolding parent, like someone from the cast of *Friends*. I regretted the words immediately. By the time class had begun, I'd apologized to Paul, had made my best attempts to take back those words. I was ashamed for losing my temper, for attempting a lame joke that made me disappointed in myself more than anything.

Four months later, he was diagnosed with cancer. Two years later he was dead.

We had a conversation online about it, maybe one year later. Somehow I'd managed to bring it up. He remembered what I'd said, and he accepted my apology and told me it wasn't my fault. That I shouldn't think anything of it.

Right, of course, I'd think.

I would thank him, and I would pray for him, but he wouldn't live.

∿∿∿∿

From diary entry, 10/13/2005—Biloxi, MS

The lights are on as we go back to the stadium. One-mile walk and it feels good, though my feet are tired... The sun set before we left. The sun was burning red and the sky was a heavenly mix of pink, orange, yellow, purply hues. The sun disappeared; the moon took its place.

Showers in the dark. A white trailer in the stadium—Salvation Army provided —cold water. Finding sleeping... bags under tent with flashlights. Clean clothes. Freshness.

The destruction is unbelievable. But I get to leave. That is what is hardest. I must imagine these houses, lives, as my own, and then, only then, can I begin to understand...

℘

The dust in Pompeii is choking, and I wonder if the ashes of Vesuvius are falling again as the skies darken and rain rinses grit and grime from my face. Rose and I wait in the shelter for the train back to Rome, back to the airport, back to Ireland, listening as the wind slaps water against the walls.

The morning after the night Paul died (but before I knew about it—before I got that phone call later that evening while writing up an article at my college newspaper's office), I went for an early morning run. The sun was up, leaves of the live oaks waving in the breeze. I felt my legs push beneath me. I felt the air fresh in my lungs, I heard birds in trees and saw squirrels chasing each other across the quad.

And I thought, *How beautiful.*

How beautiful.

I stand singing a hymn in a Catholic sanctuary, incense curling up my nose, my body sensing that Jenny is crying nearby. I don't cry during the funeral—not much. It isn't until I step out the doors and into the sun—standing, staring at a black-and-white photocopy of a childhood photo of Paul on the front of the program—that my body begins to shake and heave, my eyes spill over.

When our memories are gone, are those we love gone, too? When the journals, and boxes, and books, and computers, and videotapes are all water-damaged and covered with mud, or when their owners no longer breathe, or when hundreds of years have gone by, will what we have said or what we have done, who we have loved and who we have hated, who we remembered and who we let go—will any of this matter at all?

"Bodies are bodies," Mr. Myeong said. "The dead are with us no more." He was leaving from school that day for a funeral—for his father's brother. His father was long dead.

I imagined him on the way to a village near Gwangju, gathering with relatives at the family plot, small bumps pushing out of the ground.

"Time flies like an arrow," he would later say, while we're eating a final dinner, while he wishes me well on my return to the U.S. He'd talk about *jeong*—that Korean word for something that's not family and different than love, but like them—but he'd remind me that even those connections end. That meeting people part. That even parents must leave their children.

If I could, I'd send a letter to Paul. I'd write it on paper or papyrus or bowl, and I would slip it into the infinite beyond. I would tell him I'm sorry for any mean thing I ever said and that I wished I'd kissed him when I had the chance. That I remembered our first dance in eighth grade, that he was the first boy who held my hand, that at the funeral, I'm sure his mom had dressed him in one of the shirts he'd worn to Homecoming with me.

And I would tell him I miss him. Sometimes.

I've imagined what he would write back—that he misses me, too, that the weather is great in heaven, to tell everyone that he says hi.

But really, I don't know. I don't know what—if anything—he would say.

LABYRINTH

Pilgrims are persons in motion, passing through territories not their own—seeking something we might call completion, or perhaps the word clarity will do as well, a goal to which only the spirit's compass points the way. –Richard R. Niebuhr

I stand at the mouth of a labyrinth, the late morning sun a dollop of orange in the sky. A broad-brimmed hat is pulled down tight on my head, and a troupe of flies buzzes against the net that covers my face like a veil. I toe the sandy ground and look at the rocks outlining the path ahead of me. It winds forward from my feet—a single route that curves back in on itself again and again until it reaches a white gravel center.

The heat rises as the Western Australian desert sun creeps higher into the sky. I say a brief, silent prayer, the circle of the labyrinth and the spread of the wilderness before me.

I put one foot in front of the other, repeating centering words in my head—things like "grace" and "peace" and "love." I whisper-sing Taizé songs (*Come and fill our hearts with your peace; you alone, oh Lord, are holy*). I walk slowly, hemmed within the narrow path. It is simultaneously disorienting and freeing—turning back on sharp corners, getting closer to the center of the circle only to be led back to the outer edges.

I watch my feet crunching on the dirt and gravel, note the turns, stop to look up at the birds darting by, at the large Moreton Bay fig tree that guards the labyrinth's mouth.

As I move deeper into the labyrinth, heat gathers in my chest, and tears make tracks down my cheeks. It's dirty crying—snot-filled and moving through my whole body. I feel with it the weight of grief and the inexplicability of God's love. I wish I'd brought Kleenex or, as my retreat director would suggest later, a tea towel.

When I reach the center of the labyrinth, I circle around its curves and finally sit on the white gravel. A few minutes pass, or maybe twenty. It's hard to tell.

I look at the fig tree and the bright blue of the midday sky. I breathe and breathe.

*

In the Australian bush that surrounds Koora Retreat Centre, you can still find items left behind by European immigrants—a chipped teacup, the rusted seat of a tricycle. Hidden from the highway nearby, the center itself feels a little like a found object: Once you turn off the highway and onto the nondescript dirt road that leads up to the center, a series of modular homes emerges from the land, almost blending into it. The stout buildings are set up in a square, their doors facing inward to a sunny courtyard. Lizards sunbathe on stone slabs. Birds cling to the tops of trees that sway in the wind.

I arrived in February—late summer in Australia—and I was the only retreatant there. A few days before I took that first step into the labyrinth, Anna, the Anglican priest who runs the center, picked me up at the "train station" in Southern Cross—a small, raised platform and the closest stop to Koora on the seven-hour train route from Perth to Kalgoorlie. Anna met me with a quiet smile, her silver hair tucked behind her ears. I was the only one who got on or off. We both watched as the train chugged away.

We passed much of our one-hour drive to Koora in a semi-comfortable silence, the highway speeding by, the world a whir of browns and golds and oranges and a smattering of greens. She asked me about my travels, and I told her I'd been on the road for nine months, mostly in Asia. I'd considered going on retreats elsewhere—ten days of silence at a Buddhist retreat center in Nepal, or a yoga retreat in India—but they'd never worked out.

Anna told me she'd taken a similar journey decades before when she was in her forties, her kids almost grown. "Month nine is hard," she said. "I felt it. Most people go to the familiar at month nine." She laughed good-naturedly and gestured out the window. "And you come to the Australian desert."

The rusty soil blurred by as our SUV motored on. I watched it go—the flat, dry landscape like nothing I'd experienced before. The sun glared at us through the windshield.

I wanted to say that I'd been longing for a place like this. That while I'd found God throughout my journey—in shimmering golden temples and in the kindness of strangers and in the deep need to trust something more than myself—I was seeking a different kind of respite.

But I didn't say those things. Instead, I looked at the winding asphalt in front of us and gave a short nod. "Well, I think this is just what I need."

*

There are few notable landmarks in the bush, and if you get too turned around, you might not be able to find your way back. Anna and her husband Peter warned me of this early on, had ensured that I had a compass on my smartphone, had told me about the bright ribbons they'd tied on trees and bushes to mark the path. They pointed out the landmarks they could—the Moreton Bay fig, a cell phone tower far on the horizon, the huge water pipe that brought water into the desert all the way from Perth. The consequences of getting "bushed," as Peter called it, were dire: Many a European who'd come into the uninviting desert in the 1800s and 1900s had gotten himself turned around in circles, running out of food and water and soon ending his journey in death.

My first evening there, as I took a walk into the wilderness with Anna, I saw what those Europeans must have seen. The falling sun cast sharp shadows across our bodies. The world was harsh and unforgiving.

But the next morning, the desert looked different. Beneath the limbs of dead trees dried out by the sun, ants built towering hills and lizards rested in the shade. New bushes grew around dead ones, and songbirds danced among them. Tiny purple flowers pushed out of the dry soil, their bright colors sparking against the landscape's beiges and grays. A light breeze lifted away the flies. Evergreen trees waved their shimmering leaves, beckoning.

Still, as I wandered from one ribbon to the next on my own, a note of nervousness flashed through me whenever I felt like I'd gone too long without spotting one. But then I'd see a bright flash of pink or orange fluttering on the wind.

Relief flooded through me each time.

*

I left the United States the year before, at age thirty-two, driven by a depression that had tailed me for years. I could trace its seeds to many things—toxic work environments, burnout after years of engaging in anti-violence and LGBTQ advocacy in South Carolina, a sense of the Sisyphean nature of activism and social justice work—but I didn't understand it. My work was fulfilling, I had a community that supported me, and I had loved ones who warmed my heart.

Still, dishes piled up in my sink. Stacks of papers grew into mountain ranges in my bedroom. Around me, a thickness pressed in. As if through water, I tried to swim. But my limbs shifted slowly, and my brain moved even slower. I found myself gasping for air.

Each morning, I struggled to get up, to find the words to convince people that queer lives and trans lives and Black lives and women's lives mattered. To convince the hierarchies around me that I mattered.

I thought often about death but wrote in my journal that I couldn't or wouldn't do it—that I valued life too much to take my own—but the words seem wooden when I read them now, like perhaps I was trying to convince myself they were true.

God, something has to change, I wrote.

Then one day, when my depression was at its worst, my friend Keyes took me on a drive.

Rain was coming down in sheets, the klaxons blaring on the radio, the windshield wipers beating wildly back and forth. Keyes pulled over into a parking lot by an empty park. Streetlights cast strange shadows on my skin, the water making the light shift and change. I swallowed down the heat that had gathered in my throat.

"I just—I don't know how to go on," I said. "But then I ran across this blog, and this person sold all their stuff and traveled—for months, for years, even—and something inside me said, 'I want to do that.' I know it's crazy, but—"

"It's not crazy," Keyes said.

I paused, unsure if I'd heard him right. "It's not?"

*

In the Australian desert, there are these trees that grow in the wilderness and have this beautiful, burnt orange bark, and their arms twist up to the sky, and when I went on my daily walks in the desert, I couldn't stop looking at them. But it's not the trees' beautiful form that drew me to them.

I stared because they were full of dead branches. Lots of living ones, of course, but every rung up or so, out of those beautiful, smooth branches came one that was desiccated and gray. But the tree just kept growing around them, higher and greener and more alive.

It was a matter of survival, Anna told me. When the tree doesn't have enough resources to feed all its branches, it stops sending food and water to one of them—but then the rest can keep growing.

The dead branches don't fall. The tree just holds onto them, and birds build nests in their nooks and crannies, and passersby can rest in their shade. They're a part of the tree—present, persisting, held.

A PORTRAIT OF MY HOMESTAY MOTHER

She sits across from me at the heavy wooden table. The remains of our dinner lie between us—sticky smudges and pale rings. Bits of dried seaweed, a stray grain of rice. Moments before, we ate together from dishes that sat in the table's center—the traditional Korean style—spooning soup from thick black bowls, pulling flakes of fish off bone, and plucking bean sprouts from small bowls of *banchan*.

This particular night could be many nights—the bowls, the steam, the metal chopsticks that slip between my fingertips even months after I moved to Korea. The meal is over, and we are sitting in silence as the green tea steeps—and then, she pours some into my small, waiting cup.

The earthy flavor slips over my tongue, settling warm in my stomach. Night has fallen, and her teenage daughter is somewhere else—probably one of the *hagwons* she studies at each night. Her college-aged son—a few years younger than I am—is elsewhere, serving his mandatory two years with the military. Her husband is probably working at the little convenience store they manage—the one on the edge of Dolsan Park, a nudge of a foothill that borders the sea.

She will go later to the store—to work with her husband or to relieve him of his duties. Or perhaps she is done for the night, and she'll suggest we go for a walk or to the sauna.

Once, she told me not to lean back and stretch in my chair after a meal. *Your spirit will fly away*, she told me. Another time, her eyes went wide when I whistled on one of our nighttime walks. *Whistling at night attracts ghosts*, she said.

It took several tries to communicate this, though. I didn't know the Korean word for "ghost," and she didn't know the English one. Hand gestures ensued, and other words—words about words, most of which we didn't understand. Eventually, she made a ghostly sound—*ooooo*—and waved her hands around.

"Ohhh," I said. "*Ghosts!*"

We both laughed as I repeated the word in Korean, and she took on my English.

Now, she sits at the table sipping tea, her short black hair tucked behind her ears and flecked with strands of gray. She looks up, the smile lines around her eyes crinkling. In each of our hands is a small Korean-English dictionary.

She says something to me in Korean or, perhaps, asks a question—but I only understand half of it. So, she tries again in English but gets stuck on a missing word. Her fingers rummage through the onion-skin pages of the dictionary until she finds it—*dream* or *career* or *military*. Perhaps it's something about my family, or God, or my future, or her past. Perhaps it's just about my day teaching at her daughter's school, or maybe it's about her weekend plans.

In turn, I answer, the Korean words like marbles in my mouth. I, too, pinch the dictionary's thin pages, trying to find—

My brown curly hair and blue eyes mark me as Other here—*oeguk*, a foreigner. I teach high schoolers the difference between *l* and *r*, but I stumble over words whenever I speak Korean. In the teachers' shared office, I make jokes with my neighboring coworker, who is kind and funny and very good at English.

But still, I feel so lonely sometimes.

And then, there is this, here. My homestay mother smiling at me, the whisper of the pages, her laughter glowing in the night.

Years later, when I am in the United States, she and her daughter will send me video messages. She will speak Korean slowly and simply, her accent and intonation like a song I once knew, something familiar and beloved. Something I thought I had forgotten—and still, I understand.

EATING TURTLE

The sweet-salty broth on my lips.

The winding streets of Taipei, the skyscrapers giving way to stout homes.

The incense in my hands, three sticks, walking up to three altars for three deities, placing a stick at each one. Praying for safe travels, for my friends who are sick or hurting, for my future.

The stinky tofu vendor on the corner, words tumbling out of my mouth, hoping I don't get them wrong.

That first day there, sweat at my temples, feet pounding on the sidewalk, trying to find a place with a menu in English. Eating by myself on a hard plastic chair, hard table beneath my elbows, slurping down noodles, watching the faces pass.

And later, a turtle in your throat—those feelings you can't say—and the steam rising up from our teas as we look across the table at each other.

You ask me what I want—what I want to order.

"What do you recommend?" I say.

You always seem to have an answer.

*

When a mutual friend—a young Taiwanese man I met while traveling in South Korea the year before—introduced us over Facebook Messenger, I was wary. I remembered how it had been my first year teaching in South Korea when I was twenty-two, all those strangers wanting to meet me. As a foreigner in rural Korea in 2006, I was a unique addition to anyone's social circle, and my language was a hot commodity. Everyone wanted to learn English, and if they didn't, they wanted their kids to. Families took me on daytrips to show me the countryside and chat with their middle schoolers in English. Koreans who had lived abroad took me out to coffee—both because they remembered what it was like to be a stranger in a strange land and also because their English was getting rusty and they wanted—they wanted—

Everyone wanted something. The lonely forty-something with a struggling marriage, the father with ambitious plans for his kid's future, the social worker in her mid-thirties who lived at home with her aging father and had watched her life slip by—except for those times when she traveled to India or Canada or anywhere else but the small city of Yeosu where we both lived.

In each case, we both benefited from these symbiotic relationships. I was a lonely foreigner in need of friends, and there were all these folks who wanted to connect. But several months into that adventure, sometimes I couldn't tell anymore: Who wanted to know me for me, and who only wanted an English tutor?

And what did I really want?

*

I wait to meet you at the bottom of Taipei 101, a gleaming tower that juts above the city's skyline. I stand just outside of the subway stop's entrance as throngs of visitors bustle by me on their way to dinner or home or another spot on Taipei's tourist trail. Neon lights from the tower blink down. An escalator carries people up into the darkness, and at the top, they disappear over the edge and into the sky. As face after face floats down on the other escalator, I realize I don't know what you look like.

And I still can't figure out why you want to hang out with me. And as for me, I'm no longer the stereotypical young American woman I was when I first lived in Asia. In the intervening ten years, I've cut my hair short, started wearing men's clothes, donned a chest binder, and come out as loudly and proudly queer—and, within the last year, nonbinary. Loud and proud, that is, except in foreign countries sometimes, and with people I don't know, and—

You find me at the bottom of the escalator. You recognize me first, but then again, my foreignness sometimes makes me stand out. Your greeting is quiet, your English cautious but impeccable.

You point to the glimmering tower. "Are you hungry?"

*

Inside Taipei 101, you add our names to the list of waiting customers at Din Tai Fung, the world-famous *xiao long bao* (Taiwanese soup dumplings) restaurant. The hostess tells you the wait will be about an hour, and so we walk into the mall that occupies the bottom few floors of the tower. The floor glistens beneath our feet. We wend our way through the twists and turns. Most of the shops are closed, but their wares shine at us along with images of happy people with sparkling watches and mannequins with pressed shirts. You ask me about my travels. I tell you I've been on the road for almost a year, that I've traveled to thirteen countries in that time, that I haven't seen my family or friends in the U.S. since I left the year before.

You wonder aloud at how good and bad it must be to travel so far and so long alone. "Did you get lonely?" you ask.

I don't know how to answer. "Sometimes," I say. "But every month or so, I'd meet up with someone I knew. A couple friends took vacations to travel with me. In Myanmar, I met up with an old buddy from college who was teaching in Yangon. And I stayed with my Korean homestay sister in Seoul—the one I lived with when I taught there—for almost three months last summer. And, you know, I've met so many kind people along the way."

You stare at the ground for a moment and then look back at me, your face serious. "You must see the world in a different way now. From when you left."

I nod. "We are all so small," I say. "But so connected."

*

I didn't come out to my homestay sister Boyeon until I had to. The year before I traveled to Taipei, I stayed in her one-bedroom apartment in Seoul all summer—sharing a *yo*, a Korean sleeping mat, like we were at a months-long slumber party. She was in her twenties—a far cry from the shy sixteen-year-old I'd met ten years before in Yeosu—and I knew she was open-minded. But anti-LGBTQ sentiment runs strong in South Korea, especially among Korean Christians. And she was Christian, and we were sharing a bed. What if she freaked out or I made her uncomfortable? Or what if it changed everything between us—this bond we'd forged over ten years?

After that summer together in Seoul, she accompanied me on the first leg of my world travels. We were on our way to southern India. We had an overnight layover in Bangkok and were staying in a hostel, sharing a bed. When we'd settled in for the evening, snuggled under the covers, she asked me about how I dressed—when I started wearing men's clothes and why. I told her a little about my gender journey—how I'd been a tomboy as a kid, how I tried to fit in with the other girls in high school and college, how, in my late twenties, I ultimately realized my masculinity was a beautiful part of who I was and am. And how I'd hesitated to express that because, in the past, I'd been afraid that I'd never find a boyfriend if I did.

But there was one part of the story I wasn't telling her: How dating women and other queer folks had made that transition easier. How the people I dated now found my gender nonconformity more attractive than off-putting.

I cleared my throat. "So… you know I don't just date men, right?"

She gave me a quizzical look.

"I date women, too. And other people who don't identify as men."

She looked at me, her expression unreadable. "No, I didn't know."

I shifted my gaze to the ceiling and launched back into my explanation of my gender, eager to get away from the subject of my queerness.

As we went to bed that night, I wondered if things would be different in the morning—if, once she processed this revelation, I'd see a hitch in her affections.

But I found in the morning that nothing had changed. And nothing changed during our trip. She still linked her arm in mine as we walked down the street. She still put her head on my shoulder when we had long, serious talks into the night.

She still loved me as much as she ever had.

*

During our dinner, there in the middle of Din Tai Fung, over the steaming plates of dumplings and green leaves of morning glory that are cooked to silky perfection, you come out to me. You tell me about your partner—your girlfriend—and the problems you're having. You tell me how you almost didn't meet me that night because you'd just had a terrible argument. How you love each other and live together, but maybe it's ending.

There is something to the words you give to me then. Something in your trust.

We eat until our stomachs are full and speak until our tongues are tired.

"I am glad I came here," you tell me as the server clears our plates. "I was so sad before I arrived because of things with my girlfriend. But I'm grateful to have spent this time with you. It is what I needed, I think."

"Me, too," I say.

You pause, looking at me with a small smile. "Talking with you—it's like looking in a mirror, but different."

*

In the days that follow, you introduce me to your brother first, and then your other friends and your girlfriend. We gather around large tables in local restaurants and eat meats and greens and ladle soups from shared bowls. We do a tea tasting in a tea shop, sipping from small cups and glasses. A few days later, I am on a train that is taking me out of the city.

You have to work, but your friends and your girlfriend and your brother guide me into the beautiful, rolling hillsides of your island nation. We stop in a town where tourists release paper balloons with messages of hope scrawled across them. It is a small town, and the balloons are released along the railroad tracks, and up they fly into the sky, each color representing a different kind of wish—for love, for money, for peace. I see one that says "health and wealth" written in Korean. On another, "Impeach Trump" is scrawled in big block letters in English. We watch as they float higher and higher into the bright blue sky above us.

I eat candy your friends buy from a corner store—one with old stuff they used to get when they were kids—and they tell me stories about them, stories and memories, there as the snacks crunch in our mouths and candies melt together on our tongues, sweet and hard.

Later, you take me to a bubble tea café, supposedly one of the original ones, and everyone is there—your friends and your girlfriend and your brother, and even the mutual friend who introduced us, who came out from behind his books and came out to me as well, and somehow here we are, this rainbow-tinged crowd of sorts. I sip on my sweet milk tea through a fat straw, the tapioca *boba* popping into my mouth. Their chewy texture sticks to my teeth, and I drink down the tea to wash it away.

You ask me if I have a Korean name. I tell you I was given one once, but I'd forgotten it. Instead, I write my name in Korean characters: 알렉시스 (al-leg-shi-seu). You and your friends brainstorm names for me using Chinese characters. You discuss the options like you're figuring out a puzzle, or perhaps a little like Goldilocks—one name is too feminine, another too masculine—before landing on a few that could go either way. That represent things like strength and intelligence and kindness. You write the names on the back of a coaster and hand it to me. I trace their lines with my fingertips. When we stand to leave, I slip the coaster into my back pocket.

*

My gender was a constant source of confusion for others as I traveled. In New Delhi, I was asked to leave the women's subway car. In Korea, in an airport bathroom, an older woman looked me up and down and said to a bystander in Korean, "Is that a man or a woman?" I smiled at her and said in Korean, "I'm a woman." She quickly apologized. When this happened again in Ho Chi Minh City (one of the staff members at a railway station tried to guide me to the men's restroom), I didn't have the willpower or Vietnamese skill to respond, so I just went outside, hailed a cab, and waited until I got to my hostel to pee.

Still, I found pockets of acceptance where I could—at the Seoul Pride festival, in a lesbian bar in Singapore, at an LGBTQ-friendly Anglican retreat center in the Australian desert, with a pair of queer folks who happened to run a guesthouse in rural Vietnam.

And I traveled with queer friends, too. Over Christmas, I traveled with one of my best friends, Jen, through Singapore and Malaysia. We had dated years before but became closer as exes than we ever were as partners. In Kuala Lumpur, vibrant displays of lights lit up stores and street corners with bows and boxes and snowflakes and Christmas trees, though we sweated through our clothes in the hot afternoons. On our first evening there, we wandered through the crowds that were gathering along the Jalan Alor Food Street and ate dumplings and pork buns and rice and noodles and soup and meats cooked in savory sauces.

When we got back to the hostel, one of the staff members handed us the laundry we'd asked them to do when we first arrived. As we sorted our clothes in our small room, I found that my shirts were covered in red stains. They had washed my clothes with the laundry bag I'd been using —a red canvas bag I'd picked up on a tour in India. It had bled all over everything.

Before arriving in Malaysia, I'd put my dirty clothes in a reusable bag

I'd picked up at Creating Change, a national conference for queer and trans activists, but since it said "LGBTQ Task Force" on it, I'd switched it out for the other bag after we arrived in Kuala Lumpur. I looked queer enough as it was, I thought, but there was no need for me to advertise it.

I joked with Jen that being queer had ruined my clothes, but she didn't find my joke funny. It wasn't until later that she told me why.

"I didn't want to tell you before," she said, "but the manager who we gave our clothes to that first day? I overheard him tell some of the other staff members, 'I'm doing the homosexuals' laundry, and it smells like big fish.'" She shook her head. "I wondered if they ruined your clothing on purpose."

"Maybe they were just careless," I said.

I thought over her words in the months that followed, though. I had tried to hide who I was—at least in part—but had failed. By cutting my hair short, by wearing men's clothes, by wearing a chest binder, was I putting myself—and my travel companions—at risk?

I became more cautious each time I went to a new country. Despite the connectedness I felt to so many around me, I knew it wasn't always safe to be myself.

*

We sit together in a coffeeshop the last evening I'm in Taipei. The coffeeshop is called Fika Fika, a Swedish word that's about drinking coffee together but also about taking the time—pausing—to be with the people you love. So much of our time together has been over meals, and you tell me how much food means in Taiwanese culture and in the Chinese language. For example, you say, the phrase "eating grass" means getting back together with an ex. Another phrase involving grass means moving on from an ex. If someone is "eating humans," they're selfish.

And there's another phrase, you say. "Eating turtle." It's when your emotions get stuck in your throat. You can't say the things you want to say, and it's frustrating—but the words get stuck because they're too full of feeling.

You tell me we have only known each other for a short time, but you and your friends—in one week, we have become so close. But you don't know how to express, how to say—

*

In the morning, before I take the train to the Taipei airport, I meet you and one of your friends for one more meal. We return to your place after—a one-room apartment with space mostly taken up by a large piano. You and your partner are musicians. I meet your cat, and you make us tea, and your friend asks about your partner and how things are going, and we play a game of Chinese checkers on your phone.

Your friend says something to you in Chinese, and you smile sadly.

"It's about saying goodbye," you say, gesturing to your friend, who has somehow become my friend.

"We have a saying," she says. "Every meal must end."

You nod slowly. "But how do you deal with knowing every meal must end?"

*

When I lived in Korea, my co-teacher, and others I grew to love there, told me of the thin red threads that connect our hearts together— that connect us to those we love from one lifetime to the next. As a white person who practices Christianity (but is influenced by Buddhism, the Desert Mothers and Fathers and Christian mystics, and other faith and spiritual traditions), I feel a little odd repeating these kinds of words. It is not my concept to share, and yet the love I felt there was real, and the threads they told me about make sense.

Besides, how else do you explain it? That feeling you have that you've known someone before? That tug that pulls you to somewhere far away —another country, another land—only to feel more at home than you ever did in your own country?

*

I remember meeting you at the bottom of that escalator, how you seemed shy at first, but then the words flowed out like promises. For so many of these months of traveling, I'd hidden—hidden these parts of myself from a world in which I didn't know if I was safe to be me. I had met such kind people along the way, but this was something different.

My glasses steamed up over the boiling hot pots, you filled our tables with local delicacies, and you told me what they were and that they were the best at each place we went. You welcomed me in. You made me a home.

In Korean, there's a word for that kind of connection, a love beyond space and time, beyond family (though it often includes family)—this bond that latches one to another. Koreans have this word, *jeong*, and the Taiwanese have all these phrases about food. But in English there's only "love," there's only this one word, but I want so many words—I want something to describe the force that draws me across oceans, what it means to find people you can bring your whole self to, how it feels when you say goodbye to someone you're certain you've known for lifetimes. But the words aren't there, and the feelings get stuck in my throat.

"We will meet again," I say the morning I leave.

"We will," you answer.

And somehow, I know it to be true.

ACKNOWLEDGMENTS

I am grateful to the following for publishing the essays included in *Eating Turtle*:

- "In the Shadow of the Taj," *Wanderlust: A Travel Journal*, Fall 2018
- "Talking with the Dead," *Oyez Review*, Spring 2013
- "Labyrinth," *Relief*, Fall 2023
- "Eating Turtle," *Allegory Ridge*, 2019

Alexis Stratton has an MFA in Creative Writing from the University of South Carolina in Columbia, SC, and their stories and essays have appeared in *storySouth, Hayden's Ferry Review, Matador Review,* and *Oyez Review,* among other publications. In 2022, their fiction chapbook *Anywhere Else but Here* was published by *Fjords Review,* and in 2024, they published *Trans Kids, Our Kids: Stories and Resources from the Frontlines of the Movement for Transgender Youth* (Ig Publishing, co-authored with Adam Polaski and Jasmine Beach-Ferrara). Alexis lives in Richmond, VA, where they work as a freelance writer and an LGBTQ rights advocate.

ABOUT SMALL HARBOR PUBLISHING

Small Harbor Publishing is a 501c3 nonprofit organization. Our goal is to publish unique and diverse voices. We are a feminist press, and we are committed to diversity and inclusion. We strive to bring new voices to a devoted and expanding readership.

Small Harbor Publishing began in 2018 with the first issue of *Harbor Review*. The magazine is an online space where poetry and art converse. *Harbor Review* quickly grew and now publishes reviews and runs multiple micro chapbook competitions, including the Washburn Prize and the Editor's Prize.

In July 2020, Small Harbor Publishing was officially incorporated and began Harbor Editions. Harbor Editions accepts submissions through a chapbook open reading period, a hybrid chapbook open reading period, the Marginalia Series, and the Laureate Prize.

In 2023, Harbor Anthologies began with a mission to promote texts that explore social justice issues and highlight marginalized writers.

If you would like to support Small Harbor Publishing, visit our "About" page at: smallharborpublishing.com/about.